How to Build an Engaged Workforce

Also by Mack Munro

BossTalk: What Every Boss Needs to Know to About Giving Great Presentations

How to Build Better Bosses

How to Win at Performance Management

How to Be a Great Boss

How to Build an Engaged Workforce

By
Mack Munro

First Edition

KDP . Vanleer, TN

How to Build an Engaged Workforce

Published by KDP

ISBN 9781090327987

Printed in the United States of America

Illustrated by
Reuben Smith
www.scribblesetc.com

Quantity discounts are available on bulk purchases of this book for educational training purposes, fund-raising, or gift giving. For more information, contact us at the address below. Special books, booklets, or book excerpts can also be created to fit your specific needs. For more information, contact Marketing Department
P.O. Box 75, Vanleer, TN 37181

For all those managers who take the extra time each day to connect with their employees and show an interest in their Little Known Facts...

What makes a superstar employee?

They don't whine
They don't fuss
They never say "it's not my job"

They're hard to find so if you have one, you'd better figure out ways to keep them!

In order to get the most out of this book:

- Develop a deep, driving desire to master the principles inside.
- As you read, stop frequently to ask yourself how you can apply each suggestion.
- Underline or highlight important ideas.
- Review this book each month.
- Apply these principles at every opportunity. Use this book as a working handbook to guide you with your everyday management issues.
- Check up each week on the progress you're making. Ask yourself what mistakes you've made, what improvements, and what lessons you can use in the future.
- Jot down your reflections in the margins. Wrestle with the *Points to Ponder* at the end of each chapter. Be sure to date your entries and use them as a starting point in your journey to grow as a leader.

People don't care about how much you know…they want to know how much you care (about them!)

Mack Munro

Table of Contents

Preface 11

Acknowledgements 15

Chapter 1: The Power of Engagement 17

Chapter 2: Little-Know Facts: The Little-Known Secret of Motivation and Managerial Success 25

Chapter 3: *Just Be Glad You Have a Job*: The Lazy-Assed Motivation Panacea 31

Chapter 4: Communicate Early and Often 37

Chapter 5: Think of Training as an Investment 43

Chapter 6: Peek-a-boo...I See You 51

Chapter 7: Celebrate! 55

Chapter 8: The Powerful Impact of Performance Management 59

Chapter 9: Show Some Empathy! 83

Chapter 10: *"To Infinity, and Beyond!"* 91

Chapter 11: Final Thoughts 95

Appendix – Survey Findings and other resources 99

About the Author 128

Boss Builders 131

Are you taking the time to build your management skills? Read for 1 hour per day on any topic and you'll be an expert. Time to get busy!

Mack Munro

Preface

In a county courthouse in Anywhere, USA, an excited young couple is waiting in line for a marriage license. The long wait is irrelevant to them. This is a wonderful time and a lifetime of love and companionship awaits them. Two courtrooms away, a bitter couple in the midst of a divorce hearing is bickering over who gets to keep the Elvis Presley bobble head collection. Insults and expletives are hurled between the two and an exasperated judge is forced to tell the couple to behave like adults.

In a busy human resources office at a large financial firm, a recruiter is giving a verbal job offer over the phone to an excited and relieved candidate on the other end. She can barely contain herself as this position was her "dream" job. Two offices over, the Employee Relations consultant is doing an exit interview with a disgruntled employee who describes his job and his boss as emanating "straight from hell."

Both scenarios beg the question: What Happened? How can both marriage and employment begin with such promise only to wind up in a state of conflict, anger, and hatred? Is it possible that the reason people enter and leave relationships is the same reason they enter and leave a job?

People seek relationships in order to attain a level of companionship that involves a reciprocal exchange of nurturing and affection. While they seek employment for compensation, they also thrive in a workplace situation where their employer creates opportunities for them to grow personally and professionally in a healthy, collegial environment. When their partner in either situation fails to live up to their end of the agreement, the relationship is doomed to fail. What's more interesting is that, based on my research, men and women view the reasons for the end of personal and workplace relationships very differently. If you want to see the full details, check out the Appendix at the back of this book.

In 1997, McKinsey & Company commissioned a study and wrote a seminal work regarding an upcoming "War for Talent." In it, they detailed a number of factors which included an aging workforce, increasingly complex technologies, and global competition as reasons why the United States would be embroiled in (and possibly losing) this war. They revisited their work in 2001 and presented updated data that made the situation and consequences even graver.

This prompted a great many CEOs and HR executives to develop strategies to preemptively strike back with incentive and perquisite programs aimed at recruiting and retaining talent. Who could have imagined the war would take a dramatic turn with the Great Recession that began in 2008?

The economic climate at the time of this revision is improving. Even still, employees get laid off each day and thousands more are desperately seeking fewer and fewer good-paying jobs. Families are forced to scale back spending and people are anxiously awaiting better days, which may or may not get here soon.

Then there are those lucky few who never lost their jobs.

Actually, they're the focus of this book. With everyone paying attention to the bad economy and lamenting not having a job, those who are still employed are in many cases overworked and underappreciated.

If history serves, after each recession comes a mass exodus of those same overworked and underappreciated employees. They come to work each day and do their jobs, plus those held by the workers who were let go. Their only motivation during those tough days is fear and the constant exhortation of "just be thankful you have a job."

What if I told you there was a way to keep your best workers when the good times return? What if you found out it really was pretty simple and didn't cost much at all? Sometimes the secrets to solving enormous problems are just simple things done on a consistent basis. In this case, I've narrowed the steps to just a few. Take them seriously (and that means implement them!) and you'll stand a very good chance of keeping your best performers when the recession ends AND get them to perform remarkably for you right now.

Oh, and in case you don't know this, the "War for Talent" is still on. It may be a little more covert and less reported on, but the consequences for losing it are higher now than in 2000 and 1997. Superstar employees are in demand in all critical skill levels. They always will be. You can complain about the ones who were hired by someone other than you, but if hire a bunch of losers, you own them! Be prepared to fight the war conventionally and non-conventionally. Fight to win or you'll lose bigger than ever. I'll show you how to win the battles and the war.

Enjoy the read!

Acknowledgements

As in all my other books, it's the people behind the stories and experiences that make it worth reading. This book is no exception. The more I travel and work with organizations, the more I learn and in turn, can offer to teach. Every story is true even though the names may have been changed. This book is a reflection of many and to all of you, I am thankful!

If you don't have a heart for people, find another career! Management is NOT for you!

Mack Munro

Chapter 1 – The Power of Engagement

Many years ago, my ex-brother-in-law was making final preparations and plans before his bachelor party when he solemnly asked me and his Best Man if we thought he was making the right decision marrying this particular girl.

Of course we assured him he was (although neither of us liked her nor thought she was a good choice) but he persisted to probe us for our opinion. Reluctantly, we finally shared our misgivings. He seemed relieved that we supported his thoughts, but when we told him to cancel the event, he pushed back.

"No, we booked the honeymoon, the invites have gone, in-laws flew in, and it would be totally embarrassing," he said. "We've already made plans so I need to go through with it. It would be too much to call off the wedding."

In retrospect, he's probably kicked himself multiple times for not listening to us. As it happened, the marriage was a short-lived nightmare. Fortunately, they didn't stay together long enough to have children and now, as far as I know, he's remarried and happy. Of course, if you read that he's my EX-brother-in-law, you know that I also failed to heed good advice because of a litany of pre-wedding preparations. Fortunately, that marriage did result in two wonderful adult children who are now very much in my heart and mind at all times.

What does this have to do with employee satisfaction? Everything, for it shows the power of engagement.

I spend at least 35 weeks out of the year doing consulting and management training all around the United States and beyond. Over the past few years, much of that training involves keeping people happy in spite of tight economic times which often result in mandatory furlough days, cancelled or deferred bonuses, and no salary increases. Managers now are desperately trying to keep their people loyal so they'll at least hang in there until the cash flow comes back. In most cases, they're fighting an uphill battle. That is unless they focus their attention on engagement.

Engagement is a commitment, almost a contract between two people. It's a promise that they'll agree to make it to a designated milestone (a wedding) and plan diligently to live together beyond that date. When people become engaged, they begin to make long-term plans. Sometimes they'll combine their bank accounts, buy houses together, and start thinking strategically about tough issues such as raising children, religion, and where they may choose to live. In preparation for the wedding, they buy rings, dresses, rent hotel ballrooms, and book a honeymoon destination. Then to further set it in stone, they register for gifts and send out the invitations. As distant family and friends RSVP and book their flights, the commitment deepens. Then gifts begin arriving. As the day draws closer, the rational choice becomes clearer: The wedding is a go!

Logically of course they could tap out at any time, but in most cases, in their opinion, it's too late. Too much has been invested to turn back.

Wouldn't it be great if you could get this kind of focused, dedicated (and almost irrational) commitment from your superstar employees? Imagine if they hung in there, without whining when they got news about furloughs and smaller pay raises. Visualize an environment where people did more than "just their jobs" and actually looked for ways to make a difference. If it all sounds farfetched, let me assure you it's not, and, if you take the information in this book seriously, you can in fact have that kind of engaged workforce. To do it, you have to move people from simple job satisfaction, over the bridge of fulfillment, and into a state of engagement. Look at the figure on the next page.

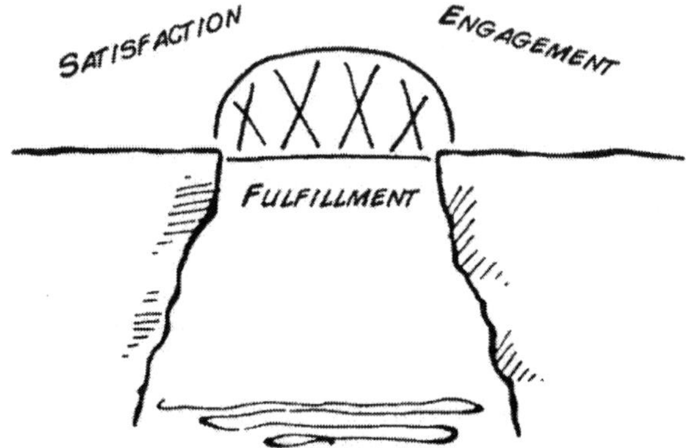

A few years ago I was teaching a three-day leadership workshop to a group of emerging leaders at a large manufacturing company in Hartford, CT. I took at cab from the Bradley Airport and stayed at a *Holiday Inn*, not far from the training facility.

Now most of the time I travel, I'll spend evenings in my hotel room working on projects and dining on room service. Yes I know it sounds boring but since my home office is really a home office, it affords me a modicum of peace I don't have at home with the chaos 32 acres, a teenaged daughter, and 3 dogs running wild.

One of my favorite foods happens to be Buffalo wings, and I was delighted to see them on the room service menu. To combat the negative health benefit of the wings and a *Guinness* or two to drink, I dutifully ordered a chicken Caesar salad as the main course. When the food arrived, I prepared myself to be completely delighted. I tipped the server and when he left, removed the metal plate warmers. What a major disappointment!

The "Buffalo wings" turned out to be cheap replicas of *McDonald's Chicken McNuggets* with some hot sauce squirted on. The chicken on the salad was burned, and the wilted lettuce came complete with the lettuce core most normal people discard. I don't know if it was some sick twisted garnishment but I didn't like it. The dressing was as scant as participants at a Baptist church dance party and to make it worse, my *Guinness* was warm. Not wanting to make a scene, I ate everything but the lettuce core and was satisfied, satisfied in that I was no longer hungry, but certainly not fulfilled.

To make matters worse, the shuttle that was to take me to the training center was out of commission, meaning I had to walk nearly a mile with lugging all my books and training materials. It seemed kind of silly calling a cab to do that short drive. Oh yes, and on the third day, it rained and I had to walk to the training site with my luggage as well.

Was I engaged to that particular *Holiday Inn*? No way! Yes I was fed and had a bed and a roof, but that satisfied only the basic needs. Other than that, it was a very unremarkable, unfulfilling experience.

By the way, when I go back there, I'm now officially engaged to the *Hilton Garden Inn* in nearby Glastonbury. Yes, I have to rent a car, but you talk about a much better environment! I rave to anyone who will listen about the great experience. I'm also engaged to *Southwest Airlines, National Car rental, Five Guys,* and any other institution that provides a flawless, remarkable, engaging, and fulfilling experience.

Are you prepared to create the kind of engaging environment in your organization? It's not easy or for the faint of heart, but well worth the effort I can assure you. The principles are very simple. Don't confuse simple with simplistic. Each one takes work. But let me assure you, if you make the effort, you'll be generously rewarded.

Engaged employees will:

- Show up early for work, not just on time.
- Do more than their job description dictates
- Stop whining and start working
- Squelch the whining of co-workers
- Think of innovative ways to make money

- Come up with creative ways to solve problems
- Become active recruiters for good talent
- Put pressure on slackers to shape up or quit
- Generally make your day 100% better!

If that sounds good to you, then read on. Better days are ahead and I want you to fully enjoy them!

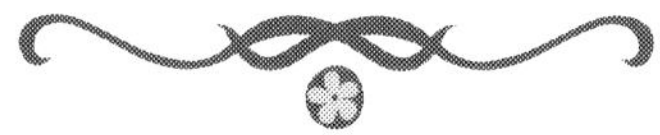

Points to Ponder

1. Do you think my thoughts on engagement are farfetched? If so, would having them become reality be a good thing for you?

2. Can you think of some of your employees right now who you'd do anything to keep? Do you fear losing them when the job market improves?

3. What would you do to keep them?

Chapter 2 – Little-Known Facts: The Little-Know Secret to Motivation and Managerial Success

Sara is a 30-year veteran of the United States Navy with a reputation as a fair, but no-nonsense manager. Her career was punctuated by remarkable accomplishment and an occasional bout of head-butting, which in nearly every case she consistently won because of her attention to detail and photographic memory for people and events. Although she is now retired, her influence is felt in her community and she'll no doubt leave a legacy that future medical logisticians will be well-advised to emulate.

Having known Sara personally and professionally since 1989, I was intrigued back in 2002 when she told me of her upcoming orders to the supply department of one of the "Big Three" Naval Medical facilities. Now this particular facility had a pretty bad reputation. There were about 120 civilian employees who for the most part gravitated back and forth between apathy and aggression. She also had to manage a moderately motivated enlisted team and some extremely lazy Supply Corps officers. By all accounts, this was a challenging assignment.

Knowing Sara is one who'd argue with a Stop Sign if you let her, I prepared myself to witness the *Battle of the Century: A Contest between the Immovable Force vs. the Immovable Forces. No stopping for blood.* The ultimate *"I Quit"* match. Vince McMahon and Dana White couldn't run a Pay-Per-View to rival this one.

Much to my surprise, Sara took a different approach. The battle I couldn't wait to see never materialized. There were no brawls or riots. Sara never kicked in doors or threw things. AND, to punctuate all this, when she transferred two years later, she received more coffee cups, cards, flowers, pictures, and baskets of lotion from the *Bath and Body Works* than I'd ever seen. People were in tears. They begged her not to leave. Shortly before her actual retirement date, one of her former employees wanted to know when she was retiring. Sara's old position was becoming "civilianized" and the woman wanted to know if she would be interested. That way, she said, "you'd never have to leave us again."

Just a few little-known facts.

You see, what Sara did on her first few weeks was make the rounds in the Cube Farm talking to the staff. She chatted with them, asking them about the pictures, trinkets, and plants that decorated their cubicles. She asked them about their dreams and their families. This took an enormous time commitment for her, but she saw it as absolutely necessary. It was an important investment into the emotional bank accounts of that tough bunch of Federal employees.

Now, lest you think it was all rosy, let me assure you it wasn't. Within the first week, one particularly sluggardly employee filed an unfounded EEO complaint as a "shot across the bow" which temporarily interrupted Sara's love fest. She also had to deal with the sense of entitlement from the officer and senior enlisted community, and battle some bullying physicians who enjoyed toying with her sanity. She did in fact have to drop the hammer on some stubborn folk, but it never became her dominant style. She never gave up, always making time to keep this emotional connection.

The ultimate key to creating a fulfilling experience that leads to engagement is to get to know your people.

I had a black lab mix named Sonny. For the most part, Sonny was a pretty good dog. He loved to run with me and when he saw me lacing up my running shoes, he started jumping around excitedly. When I reached for the leash, he went out of control.

There were times however when I needed to take Sonny someplace in the car. Same drill. He saw me getting my shoes on, saw me getting the leash, but when he saw me reach for the car keys, he paused, then turned around and ran upstairs. Usually I'd find him cowering under our king-sized bed. At that point, the only way to get him out was to throw shoes under the bed then chase him back down the stairs. Finally I managed to pick up that big black dog and put him in the car where he shook uncontrollably.

Why? Because he thought he was going to the vet. If the only time I took Sonny in the car was to see the vet, he'd always take off running.

If the only time you meet with your people is to chew on their ass, they'll scatter when they see you coming. Establishing a rapport and relationship with your people, starting with the little-known facts is the only way you'll build trust. Yes you'll have to get after them. That's totally normal. What you don't want to do is frighten them off.

Is this a breach of the traditional employer/employee relationship? No. You're not asking these people over to your house for dinner, it's just a daily check-in to see how they're doing. Investing just a few moments to show you care will pay big dividends. I suggest you start immediately. If not, nothing else in this book will work for you.

Let me repeat that. ***If you don't take the time to learn the little-known facts, nothing else in this book will work for you.***

Points to Ponder

1. Do you know the little-known facts of your team? If so, do you check in with them every day?

2. Can you think back on a boss you had that took the time to know your little-known facts? If so, how was that experience for you? Did that experience (or lack of experience) contribute to your current management style?

3. Are you willing to share your little-know facts with your team? Do you think it would encourage them to know a little more about you?

Little Known Fact about Mack:

When I was six, I was on the TV show Romper Room!

Chapter 3 – *Just Be Thankful You Have a Job:* The Lazy-Assed Motivational Panacea

Mark was a General Manager at a large manufacturing plant just outside of Philadelphia. Not the touchy-feely type, he was the last guy to give positive strokes or even a kind word. Employees knew him to be tough but fair and pretty much stayed out of his way. Fortunately, the output from this plant was a highly sought-after item that kept them running at full tilt, 24 hours a day, seven days a week.

When the recession of 2008-2009 took hold, unemployment soared in Mark's region but his plant remained fully staffed. Demand was high and Mark pushed his staff to keep the productivity rolling. Because overtime was necessary on all shifts, employees enjoyed having the spending power their friends and family members, now for the most part unemployed, could only dream about.

And yet turnover began to slowly creep up. People began resigning, a few at a time, but eventually in clusters. Alarmed at the trend, the HR department began doing exit interviews. Ironically, in most cases, these employees didn't have another job to go to, they simply wanted out. When asked why, the few that chose to answer made statements impugning Mark. This was no surprise given Mark's history and caustic management style, and seeing no other option, the HR department recommended Mark take some management training and possibly work with a coach.

I began working with Mark after meeting him in at one of my *Driving Results*™ workshops in Arlington, VA. His company contracted with me to do some coaching with him as a follow-on. It was an interesting experience.

Mark's participation in the class was miniscule. He excused himself several times to make phone calls to "put out a fire at work." When he was in the class, he sat restlessly in the back of the room, nervously bouncing on his toes as if he needed to take a leak. He only spoke up if another participant said something he didn't agree with, and then it was a little under his breath but accompanied by the look of somebody quite annoyed. His interaction with me one-on-one wasn't much different.

"I'm not sure why I'm here," he proclaimed as he plopped himself down in front of me in the empty office where we met. "When you work with a bunch of ungrateful, lazy-asses, you just gotta spell out the alternatives plain and simple – in this economy, you're lucky to have a job."

"But Mark," I replied, "Did you ever count the cost of how much you all spend recruiting and training somebody new, not to mention having to acclimate them to your plant? That cost adds up."

"Look," he countered, "most of these people are that new Generation Y or whatever you call them. They expect everything handed to them. They whine when I push them to work. Don't they realize how lucky they are to have this job? If the company can't see that, then screw 'em!"

This meeting went on for an hour and I realized there was no changing Mark's mind. I ended the meeting and reported my findings. The company tolerated Mark for another month, and then fired him. Sadly, this story doesn't have a happy ending. When dealing with human behavior, there are no guarantees.

Did Mark have a point about being lucky to have a job? Absolutely. If so, why didn't it inspire his workforce?

Yes, anyone with a job should be thankful, but trust me, this phrase doesn't motivate. It merely enforces the current reality that misery will continue so long as the bad economy does. It's too risky to find a job so tolerating poor management, long hours and stressful days is part of the price.

If you really want to say something motivating, try this:

"I'm thankful I have you working for me!"

Yeah I know it sounds touchy-feely, but try it. The act of giving them steady employment is one way to recognize them, but it won't last.

Certainly we expect our people to work hard and show some appreciation for the opportunities we give them, but please don't let this phrase be your sole source of motivation.

Your Strategy:

Try some of the following techniques to recognize your employees.

Show your appreciation for your staff's hard work each day.

Each time I eat in a certain chain of restaurants (whose parent company was of my clients) I always ask to speak to the General Manager. The server looks at me nervously as if I'm going to complain to them, but dutifully produce the GM. I then tell the GM what great service that server is giving and that they should be proud to have them on their team. It's always fun to watch the server's reaction. I hope it teaches the GM a lesson. If they're not doing this on a regular basis, that server will be gone. There's simply too much competition and turnover in that industry.

Go out of your way to catch them doing something right.

Most managers are quick to zap employees for making mistakes. Sometimes it's their natural style. Most of the time it's a behavior they learned from their manager.

How about putting a new twist on this and catch them doing something right? When you see it, say it. Tell them what they did and why you appreciate it. If not, look for your staff to avoid you when they see you coming.

Find creative ways to recognize them for specific accomplishments.

For some folks, a simple "thank you" will suffice. For others, public recognition or something tangible might work better. You'll need to build a relationship with them to discover what they want.

Think of something more motivating to say to them each day!

As we've seen, "Just be thankful you have a job" is a lazy person's way of recognizing people. Work on your technique. Highlight somebody's strengths and call them to everyone's attention. I'm convinced everybody has at least one hidden talent that provides value sometimes when you least expect it.

When I was in the Navy, I once worked with a guy who had an amazing ability to calm down angry customers and have them leave our clinic laughing and joking. You'd never know it by interacting with him on a daily basis; he could just turn it on when you needed him to. That's the kind of thing that needs to be recognized, talked about, and appreciated. Call attention to a great skill like that and you'll be sure to motivate them!

Points to Ponder

1. What statements tend to motivate you at work? Is it possible these won't motivate your staff? If not, are you still using them to motivate?

2. Think back on your favorite manager. Now reflect on the worst one you ever had. What statements did they use to motivate you? Did either manager have a profound influence on you?

3. Think about your current staff. Is there anyone you think may be on the verge of disengaging? What are you prepared to do to bring them back?

Chapter 4 – Communicate Early and Often

Years ago, I was a volunteer greeter at my church in Southern California. Now if you're not the churchgoing type, the greeters are the people who welcome you at the door and hand you a bulletin. On the fourth Sunday of the month, greeters also did double duty preparing the elements for Communion (where you remember the Last Supper, again for those of you who don't do church). This involved taking a turkey baster filled with grape juice and squirting a small amount of grape juice into some mini plastic shot glasses – over 800 of them. To do this, we had to show up early, about an hour before the service started.

One Sunday morning, I showed up early and was greeted by a staff member who mentioned there would be a "big announcement" that morning. He gave no other information. I couldn't imagine what the announcement would be but it didn't sound good. I was deep in thought when another volunteer came in the church kitchen.

"Hey Mack, did you hear about the big announcement?"

"Yeah, what's it about?" I answered?

"I don't know but I heard it has something to do with Bill."

Now Bill was one of the pastors. He was a young and energetic guy so I was kind of perplexed.

Another volunteer who joined us chimed in.

"Bill? Oh my God, Bill has a heart condition. Did you all know that?

None of us did. Immediately, another volunteer offered her piece of the puzzle.

"Oh no, I heard that Pastor Frank had to do an emergency funeral this past Thursday."

Bill was dead. What a horrible way to start a church service!

The head usher mentioned that we needed to put a box of tissues at the end of every aisle. I noticed two of the staff members' wives hugging and crying. Here I was trying to maintain my composure as church members happily entered the service. This Sunday was going to officially suck!

As it turned out, Bill was alive and well. He actually got fired for something he did earlier that week. Yes it was sad, but at least he was still among the living. How do you explain the slippery slope of conversation that led to his apparent demise? Simple. ***In the absence of***

information, people will fill in what they don't know with what they THINK they know. This is how rumors get started and propagated.

Basic motivational theory says that people have a need for safety and security. Having multiple "unknowns" in your organization leads to stress and sub-optimization. When people feel their jobs are in danger, they'll underperform so as not to stand out and make mistakes. This often brings the very disaster they desperately try to prevent.

If you have information about the state of the company, good or bad, you need to share it with your staff. They'll find out anyway, trust me. Take time to frame the news in a way they'll understand. Let them know they have some control over the situation by performing at their best.

Your Strategy:

Communicate often.

People know when something's up. It's a natural instinct. They'll do what they can to find the information so be sure to feed that insatiable need. Have meetings with them, formal and informal. I know there are things you won't be able to share, but share what you can and let them know there is in fact some confidential information you have that you're not able to share. The more you feed that need for information, the more people will relax.

Keep communicating!

Re-read the paragraph above. This is for emphasis. It's really important!

Let your staff know all the news, not just the good stuff.

We all love to share good news. Bad news needs to come out too. Don't be a chicken butt and send it out by email. Get in front of people and tell them. Don't beat around the bush. If it's bad, let them know what they can do to change the current course. Give them hope. Read on for some suggestions…

Let them know their strong performance will lead to success – keep it up!

Several years ago, I did some outplacement work for a large company in Silver Spring, MD. This company, a year earlier, did a big layoff, terminating around 200 employees. It was a traumatic experience.

When I spoke with the HR director about the project I was doing, she mentioned that the strategy this year was to terminate about 60 employees, but rather than do it all at once, she wanted to minimize the trauma of the previous year and do a few at a time.

Ok, you don't have to be a genius to figure out the problem here do you? When people are sitting on pins and needles each day wondering who's next, they'll never focus on doing their jobs. This kind of environment leads to less risk-taking as a method of self-preservation. Ironically, risk-taking and creative thinking is what's required when a company is on the ropes.

What a bunch of morons! The very problem they sought to avoid is what their strategy created. How in the world do so many stupid people make it into decision-making executive positions?

So what should you do when faced with bad news? Don't sit there like a dummy. Get out and communicate. Show people the connection between their hard work and averting disaster. Encourage creativity and risk-taking. This a time when heroes emerge. You might find that leadership talent and skill in one of your people you can leverage later. Don't let your people become victims. Be a leader and lead them out of the crisis.

Communication is one of the most difficult skills to master, both the timing and technique, but it's going to be one of your keys to creating engagement. Get busy doing it or the message will carry on out of your control.

Points to Ponder

1. Is there some information you're holding onto right now that you're afraid to disseminate? What's holding you back?

2. Can you think about a time when your manager withheld information from your team? What did you do to get that information?

3. If your organization is "on the ropes" right now, is there something your employees can do to turn it around? If so, have you shared that with them?

Chapter 5 – Think of Training as an Investment

Recently, I worked with a company that made an enormous investment in their management training. This was in spite of slowing product sales and declining market share. When I asked the HR director how they managed to come up with the money to contract with me (which by the way is kind of a lot of money...) she said simply, "we can't afford NOT to invest in our management."

That seems strange doesn't it? As someone whose been doing a lot of training over the years, I see training budgets at the top of the "slash" list when the economy tanks. Many of my colleagues end up taking a big hit in their income and several have gone out of business and back to "working for the man." I'll tell you that when times are tough, this is the time to pay to increase skills!

What are you doing now to make training a priority in your organization? If you did, would it increase engagement? I think it would. Let's look at a little research for some validation.

In 1959, a psychologist named Frederick Herzberg along with several colleagues developed a theory about the nature of work itself. What he supposed, is that two things happen during the day at work:

1. *Employees have a list of things they like and dislike about their jobs.*

2. *Managers have to do things to either make employees like their job, or at least keep doing their job without complaining*

Herzberg determined that it was easier to fix the job than to beat the employees harder. By increasing job satisfaction, managers could perhaps put an end to dissatisfaction and turnover. This could in fact lead to engagement (although they weren't throwing that term around in the 1950s.)

Herzberg did this by asking this question: "What do people want from their jobs? He asked people to describe, in detail, situations when they felt exceptionally good or bad about their jobs. He then took the data and categorized it into factors affecting job attitudes. From these responses, Herzberg concluded that the replies people gave when they felt good about their jobs were significantly different from their replies when they felt bad.

Certain characteristics tend to be consistently related to job satisfaction and others to job dissatisfaction. Intrinsic factors, such as achievement, recognition, the work itself, responsibility, and advancement seem to be related to job satisfaction. When those questioned felt good about their work, they tended to attribute these characteristics to themselves. On the other hand, when they were dissatisfied, they tended to cite extrinsic factors, such as company policy and administration, supervision, interpersonal relations, and working conditions.

The data suggests that the opposite of satisfaction is not dissatisfaction, as was traditionally believed. Removing dissatisfying characteristics from a job doesn't make the job satisfying. Herzberg proposed that his finding indicated the existence of a dual continuum: the opposite of "Satisfaction" is "No Satisfaction," and the opposite of "Dissatisfaction" is "No Dissatisfaction."

According to Herzberg, the factors leading to job satisfaction are separate and distinct from those that lead to job dissatisfaction. Therefore, managers who seek to eliminate factors that can create job dissatisfaction can bring about peace, but not necessarily motivation. As a result, characteristics such as company policy and administration, supervision, interpersonal relations, working conditions, and salary have been characterized by Herzberg as *hygiene factors.* When they are adequate, people will not be dissatisfied; however, neither will they be satisfied. If we want to motivate people on their jobs, Herzberg suggests emphasizing achievement, recognition, the work itself, responsibility, and growth – characteristics most people find as intrinsically rewarding.

Ok, now let's put all that theory aside and get to the point: ***Investing into the professional development of employees can directly lead to job satisfaction*** (this is the Herzberg definition of satisfaction, not the East Hartford *Holiday Inn* definition by the way). You can achieve this through training.

What kinds of training are we talking about? Here are some options:

Technical. This type builds the skills to do the job effectively, and then to do it more efficiently. It can be done formally, in a classroom or online, or informally through coaching and mentoring.

Interpersonal. This training builds the skills to do the basic job skills even more efficiently. It may involve such topics as communication, both written and oral, assertiveness, anger management, teamwork, etc. This also can be done formally in the classroom or informally through coaching and mentoring

Managerial. This builds the skills to do the technical aspects of management. Although business schools give a foundation, they do little to enhance the day-to-day practical aspects. These skills may include teambuilding, conflict management, basic project management, performance appraisal writing, etc. These are best done in a classroom setting with follow on coaching.

Leadership Development. These skills move the manager from a technical "make-the-trains-run-on-time" technician to a true leader who can get people motivated and directed to achieving a goal. This again is best done in a classroom setting with significant coaching and group interaction with peers.

By the way, if you need management and leadership training in a practical, no-nonsense, results-oriented format, be sure to go to the Appendix and get information on how to get me or one of my outstanding associates to your organization to provide it. (Yeah, I know it's a shameless plug, but I promise you will more than get your money's worth!)

Your Strategy:

Don't cut your training budget!

Cut the fluff, but not training! Eliminate boondoggle conferences and association meetings. Halt subscriptions and meaningless technology but keep paying for training.

Identify new technologies to make you more competitive and find opportunities to provide formal training for your staff on those technologies.

Check with the vendors and see if they're sponsoring some MEANINGFUL conferences. Have the reps come onsite for training. Let your team look for new technologies to be efficient and see if you can leverage it.

Put together individual development plans and see if there is training that will fit.

This is part of the performance management information you'll get in a little while, but it's the action part of the performance management process. Link training to performance enhancement and you'll have an easier time justifying the purchase.

Keep in mind, when employees see you investing in them, they'll invest more of themselves. They won't care if you don't. Don't neglect training. More than ever, it's a necessity in hanging onto your superstars.

Points to Ponder

1. What's your training budget look like right now? Do you have money to spend? If so, spend it! If not, figure out where you can get more money.

2. Have you done a training needs assessment recently? If not, check out the Appendix and contact me. I'll do one for you!

3. How have previous training events gone? If they were a disaster, is that preventing you from doing more training?

Do you need to set up some training sessions for your managers and supervisors? Contact us at TheBossbuilders.com!

Chapter 6 – *Peek-a-boo…I See You*

Do you remember Sara, the Naval Officer from Chapter 2? What you don't know is that her career didn't start in the officer ranks. She was an enlisted Dental Technician for the first 15 years. Most of this time was spent as a chairside and surgical assistant, with the last few as a clinic manager and later an administrative assistant working with the assignment officers at the Bureau of Naval Personnel (BUPERS) in Millington, TN. It was during this assignment she was selected for a commission through a very competitive process.

Sara told me that when she walked the endless hallways of BUPERS, the officers and senior enlisted folks often stared past her, not making eye contact. It was as if she wasn't worth the effort to acknowledge and certainly not worth expending the effort of a simple greeting. Ironically, on the day she was officially commissioned, the same folks that ignored her in her enlisted uniform that morning happily greeted her and even offered to open the door for her that same afternoon.

If you ask me, that's pretty pathetic. Sadly, it happens every day in all kinds of organizations. It's not just a Navy problem. We often don't expend the energy for just a little courteous acknowledgement.

In his 1994 book *The Fifth Discipline Fieldbook*, author and consultant Peter Senge speaks of the tribes of northern Natal in South Africa and their friendly greeting to each other: *Sawu bona.* It literally means "I see you." If you're a member of the tribe, you answer back *Sikhona*, "I am here."

How many times have you walked past your employees without so much as an eyebrow raise or a nod? Your employees are living breathing humans who have emotional needs. One of them the need to be acknowledged! If you're trying to keep people motivated during a tough economy, you better, at a minimum, acknowledge their existence.

One of the simplest ways to engage your staff on a daily basis, again, is to connect over "little known facts." If they have hobbies, pets, children, interests outside of work, or any other thing that they get excited over, ask them about it! It's a great way to check in with them and tell them *Sawu bona.*

Your Strategy:

Take time to find out "little known facts."

We talked about this earlier. You actually have to do it now Ok?

Make time to check in with people – pay attention to how they decorate their space and talk to them about it – show interest in their pictures and trinkets.

People don't normally decorate their spaces for their own pleasure. They do it to show a part of their personality they want you to notice. How do I know this? When I worked for "the man" I decorated my office with skeletons. Not real ones, but little statues. I like them. I wanted people to notice them and ask me about them. It was an invitation for them to get to know me. Ask people about their stuff and you'll open up the dialog they've been dying to have.

Catch them doing something right.

We also talked about this earlier. It's so much easier to do this because it's a positive experience. Try it and see!

I'm passionate about this only because I've personally experienced the benefits. Please take some steps this week to add this process to your routine.

Points to Ponder

1. How long has it been since you acknowledged someone at work?

2. Is there someone on your staff you know very little about? When are you going to start a dialog with them?

3. Can you recall a time when you weren't acknowledged? Do you still harbor some animosity for that person? If so, I wonder if someone is holding that same kind of animosity for you?

Chapter 7 – Celebrate!

I once worked with a lady named Evelyn Olympia, a nurse educator at Holy Cross Hospital in Silver Spring, MD. I was employed there at the time as a management education specialist and had the privilege of being her teammate for nearly two years.

Evelyn spent over 30 years at Holy Cross., beginning her career there shortly after immigrating to Maryland from the Philippines. A self-starter, she quickly built her nursing skills and eventually moved into the education department. During her tenure, she made a practice of mentoring new nurses, particularly those who were also recent immigrants. Her counsel went beyond skills. She taught them how to invest their money and plan for the future. This however was not what made me take notice. Evelyn celebrated people! She never failed to miss a holiday, birthday, anniversary, or special event. Nobody who Evelyn knew would be able to escape her recognition.

Evelyn eventually retired and lives in Montgomery Village, Maryland where she stays in touch and checks in on me. She's one of the most special people I've ever met.

What can you learn from Evelyn? People want to be acknowledged for their work performance AND what happens outside of work.

Have you ever met someone that didn't want their birthday acknowledged? If so, you can bet that if nobody recognized it, they went home and pouted that night. People want to be noticed, you just need to do it in the way they find most motivating.

People can't help but bring their personal stuff to work so for that reason, recognizing special events makes complete sense. Take time to celebrate with them and you'll find they're more apt to engage.

Your Strategy:

Make a master list of special events for each employee.

This isn't hard to do. You just have to ask! One of the best tools I've found is a program online called Birthday Alarm. You can use it for free at *birthdayalarm.com.* Get a system and then be sure to update it regularly.

Be sure to make an effort to acknowledge these events in a manner the employee enjoys.

Not everyone enjoys public recognition. They all want to be recognized, but be sure you don't embarrass them. Get to know your people and you'll eventually figure this one out.

Take time as often as possible to call attention to somebody for great performance.

We've already covered this but it bears repeating.

In 1984 I was stationed at Naval Communications Station Harold E. Holt in Exmouth, Western Australia. My commanding officer there was a guy named Captain Pete Roder. He was amazing because he knew every sailor by name and even when we got simple promotions, like moving from E-2 to E-3. He always remembered the small stuff. I don't remember a lot about being in his command, but I do remember that part. In the grand scheme, isn't that what really matters? After all, the mission we had there changed rapidly after the Cold War ended and the base is now long gone. For all I know he's long gone too. But what he did had a lasting impact on me.

Recognizing special events takes just a moment yet the benefits are lifelong. What are you going to do now to get started?

Points to Ponder

1. When was the last time you wished one of your teammates a *Happy Birthday*?

2. Do you have a tracking system in place to mark special events?

3. Are you willing to recognize people individually? Having a monthly birthday celebration for all the birthdays that month doesn't cut it by the way!

4. Can you remember having someone in your work life that cared enough to recognize milestones? What kind of impact did that have on your current management style?

Chapter 8 – The Powerful Impact of Performance Management

Take a look at the diagram below. It's kind of a calendar but it also looks like a clock.

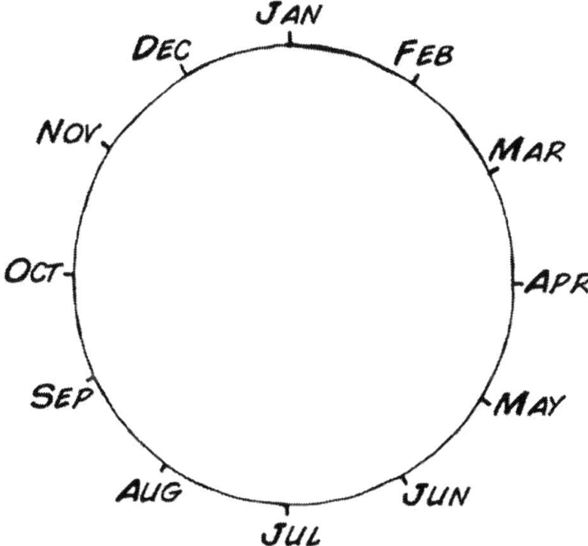

This diagram represents one year. It starts in January and ends in December.

If you were a ten-year old boy, at what point in the year would you need to be on your best behavior?

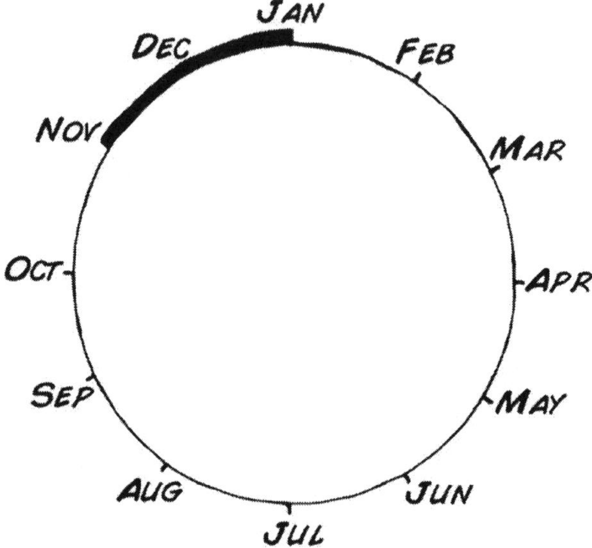

Absolutely! Just a few weeks in November and all of December. I don't care whether you celebrate Christmas, Hanukkah, or Kwanzaa. There is some sort of gift giving that takes place that last week of December.

Now, if we continue with our example using Christmas as our framework, at what time of the year would a ten-year-old boy need to be on his best behavior *IF* he believed in Santa Claus?

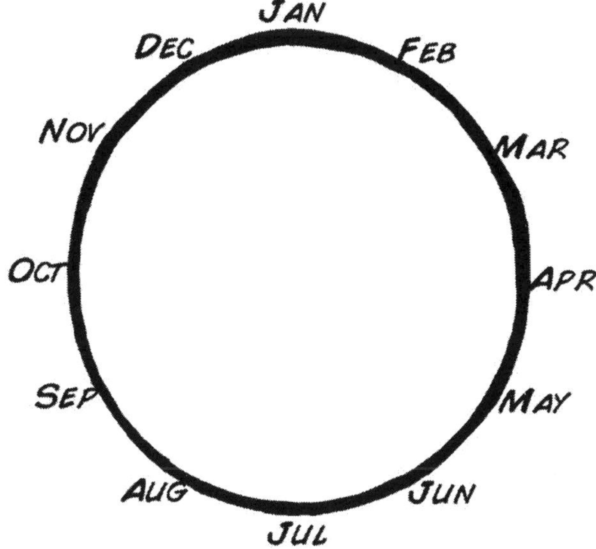

Absolutely! Year round. After all, doesn't Santa Claus know when you're sleeping, awake, blah, blah, blah?

If both boys wind up with the same gift, do you think the second boy will behave well all year long next year? No way! I wouldn't.

What does this have to do with performance management? Everything! Performance management is a daily event, punctuated by periodic evaluation. Done correctly, it results in great performance and strong engagement. People will see a reward for achieving objectives and feel more wedded to the process. Done poorly, it results in jealousy, apathy, and genuinely crappy performance. I know lots of adults that know how to turn on good performance just before appraisal time. I used to do it when I was in the Navy! That's why I'm including a significant amount of information on performance management in a book about engagement. It's a big part of it. It's the longest chapter in my book. That's a clue about how important it is.

Now, when I was a ten-year-old boy, I got a really cool toy for Christmas that year...*the Hot Wheels Power House.* Now if you're not familiar with *Hot Wheels,* they're these little metal cars that you either push around on the floor or run on some specially designed orange tracks made of flexible plastic. The tracks stick together through the use of some plastic purple "tongues" and may even include some curved pieces too. Some of you might have been spanked with one of those orange tracks. I know I was...

The *Power House* however was even more cool. It was a plastic box that sat on the track and contained little wheels inside that spun around when you plugged it into the wall. You stuck your car into the box and the *Power House* shot it around the track. It kind of looked like the diagram on the next page minus the months of the year of course.

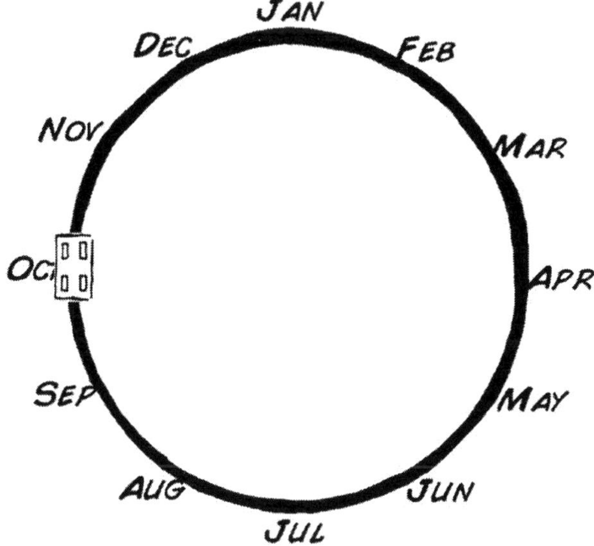

The car would go flying around the track and then slow down just before hitting the *Power House* for another shot of speed. It's kind of like what happens during a performance management cycle that's punctuated by a once-a-year appraisal. You kind of limp in for a shot of motivation.

That same year, my ten-year-old neighbor Larry got a *Power House* too (his was one of his Hanukkah gifts). He brought his over to my house and we rigged up the tracks for maximum power. Now the cars were flying around the track getting a push of power on each turn. That kept us busy for awhile, and then we got bored and flipped his *Power House* around so that the cars could crash into each other full force. That's just what ten-year-old boys do.

Can you imagine what kind of performance you could get if you actually checked in multiple times throughout the year with your employees? Look at the diagram.

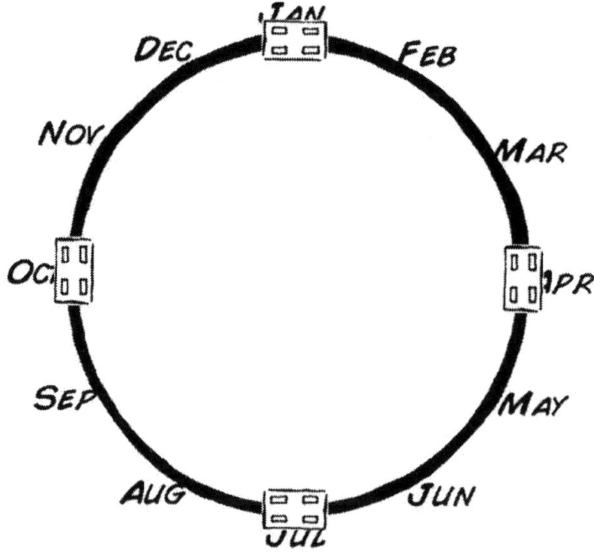

Notice that we're not talking about a formal appraisal here. The appraisal is just a tool. Real performance management is done on a frequent basis.

Now take a look at the diagram one last time. Notice what happens at each Power House meeting:

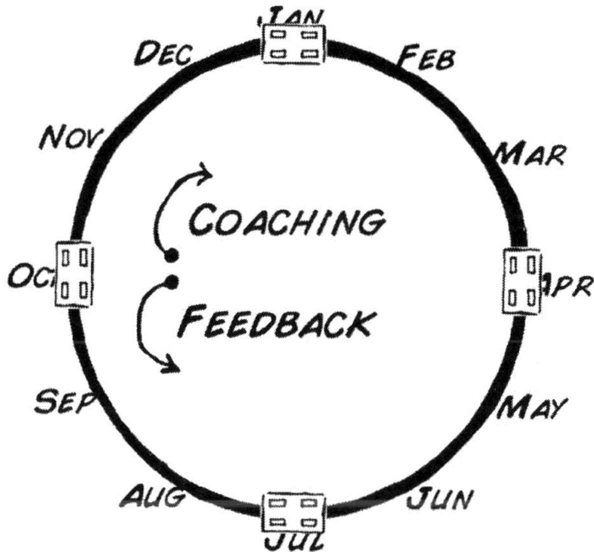

Feedback

Feedback is the act of looking back over the previous months and giving an honest assessment. Talk about what you liked and didn't like. Let that employee know in no uncertain terms what you NEVER want to see again and be clear about what you LOVED. By the way, don't wait for this meeting to correct poor performance. Do it when you see it.

Coaching

Coaching is the act of projecting forward what needs to be done in the coming months and giving some assistance. You can do this coaching yourself of find someone who may be good, relevant coach.

Sound simple enough? It really is! People need to have direction and someone along the way to keep them on task and focused on the outcome. This is the most basic and probably most important management skill. I would offer that if you chose to do just one thing as a manager, let it be performance management. If people know that what they do has an impact and really matters to you, they'll feel like they're more a part of the team and thus, more engaged.

How do you know what to give feedback and coaching on? Let's first define what makes up good performance. To do that, take a look at the next page at the *Three-Legged Stool of Great Performance*™.

In a "three-legged stool" model, all legs need to be in balance. Kick one out and you fall on your ass. Have one shorter than the other and you look like a big dummy sitting there. All need to be in balance.

The three legs here are **Skill**, **Will**, and **Focus**. Each represents a component of performance that needs to be in balance and each one also has a different impact and remedy to fix it.

Skill

Skills are the basic basics of doing a job. They can be technical or analytical. When the Skill leg is cracking, the best fix is training. We talked at length about training in Chapter 5.

Will

The Will leg becomes problematic when there are adequate skills but the person simply doesn't want to use them. We often call this an "attitude problem" and the fix is usually some kind of progressive discipline. Sometimes people use training as a fix. Don't be one of them.

A buddy of mine teaches a workshop on communicating with tact and diplomacy. He tells me the class is a tough one since most attendees get SENT to the class. Half of the class typically checks out and sits in the back playing with their smart phones. The other half are bound and determined to make everyone's experience a living hell.

Do you think the attendees KNOW how to communicate with tact and diplomacy? Of course they do. All of us learn at an early age not to tell people they're ugly or fat. They simply choose not to do it. The answer isn't training.

It's an expensive mistake to make. Don't do it. Make sure you deal with Will problems appropriately.

Focus

The Focus leg normally falters when you have a good balance of Skill and Will. Imagine if you took one of your emerging leaders to a meeting with the CEO and they began telling off-color jokes in the room. You'd want to strangle them right? They know what to do and want to do it, they're just not ready for prime time. The Focus leg is often fixed by mentoring. Let them shadow somebody who knows the ropes.

The *Three-Legged Stool of Great Performance*™ is a simple tool but rich in application. It's a guide to accurately diagnosing performance problems. You can then fix them quickly and correctly.

Sometimes though the challenge becomes figuring out how to communicate the gap between current performance and the ideal. We find it hard to pinpoint the issue. Let me see if I can help.

Here's how I currently see myself (and I think Reuben Smith did a pretty good rendition don't you?)

Now here's what I'd love to aspire to. No fear taking off my shirt at the pool if I look like this right?

Would you agree there's a significant gap between current and ideal? Absolutely! We have to fill the gap. Look at it again:

You see, the gap can be closed, but it needs some very specific actions to take place. If I'm serious about this, I'll put in the effort and invest some cash into it.

What can you do? Coach me! Encourage me! Keep me accountable! That's performance management isn't it?

Think about the folks that work for you. Are you actively checking in with them, helping them visualize what ideal performance and development looks like? Are you using empathy to close that gap from the current state? If not, you might want to get busy. Keeping performers growing and developing is a great way to keep them loyal and producing for you each day!

Many organizations aren't able to provide bonuses or increases in this tough economy and for that reason are downplaying performance management. That's the wrong move! Not everyone is motivated by money – by not tracking and managing performance you're setting the stage for failure.

How do you know your staff hits their goals when you haven't set any? Do you have any idea which employees are performing and which aren't? If you can't get a straight answer from an employee about what their working on and why it matters, you're not managing performance!

To create engagement through this process, you also have to help people increase their capacity to grow.

What's in Your Basement?

If I was planning to turn my basement into a state-of-the-art home theater, what would be the first order of business? Planning? Budgeting? Asking for permission? Buying the equipment? No.

The first order of business is to clear out the junk. After all, if you don't have the capacity to grow, you won't be able to grow. This requires you to become an active practitioner of *delegation.*

Delegation

Delegation is the act of creating the capacity for growth in yourself and others. That's my definition but I think it works. Most people push back on delegation for a host of reasons, but if you look at it as a way you can grow and also grow the skills of your employees, it will be much more palatable.

To delegate, you'll first need to create some big goals, not just for you, but also for those you're managing.

Without goals, we have nothing to shoot for; no higher purpose; nothing to look forward to. There's no motivation to do more than the absolute minimum, no urgency to push ourselves to accomplish new things, no real reason in fact to do anything more than lie on the couch and watch television all day.

Goals are an important part of identifying and landing our dream job and career. They help leverage each work experience into something new and even more exciting. It's the best way to prevent regret in your later years that you didn't accomplish more.

Goals are often thought of in terms of, well, *terms*, short term, long term, etc. While those are helpful, I'd like you to consider goals a little differently.

In 1994, Jim Collins wrote a book entitled *Built to Last – Successful Habits of Visionary Companies.* In that book, he examined companies that were successful for decades, and in some cases, centuries. These were companies that withstood economic issues, changes in culture, and even distaste in public opinion and yet always managed to survive. He gave many reasons for this longevity and backed them up with research.

One reason companies in Collins' book succeeded was that they set really good goals. Now these weren't just ordinary old goals, in fact Collins made the point that these goals far exceeded expectation and in some cases, common sense. His term for this type of goal was the *Big Hairy Audacious Goal* or the BHAG. I like this concept!

BHAGs defy logic because they're so darned grandiose. They give us something really BIG to shoot for and they define a roadmap for us to follow. They're more than just end-states. A BHAG that says "I want to be wealthy" or "I want to be happy" isn't specific. How much money is wealthy enough? How happy is happy? My thought is to define a condition or position that gives you the end-state and make that your BHAG.

Let me give you an example. My passion in life is to develop the next great generation of managers. It comes from many years toiling under some really bad ones. It was the inspiration for one of my other books, *12 Simple (but not simplistic) Principles Every Manager Needs to Know.*

Several years ago, I brainstormed a list of ways that passion could be realized and I finally decided the best way to get the message out was through mass media – my own television show. I envisioned it as a one-hour slot where I could bring bad managers up on stage, expose bad behavior, and then assist them with strategies to fix it. To me, this was a worthwhile endeavor and I made it my BHAG.

The hard part about BHAGs is that they're difficult to achieve. If they were easy, we couldn't call them BHAGs. In my case, there's no straight shot to having a TV show, so I simply envisioned the BHAG as the pinnacle of a mountain and started my journey through a series of switchbacks – diagonal trails that inch up a mountain. Take a look at the model on the next page.

Can you see how the process works? In my case, the BHAG is so big that I'll never get straight there. My career progression post-Navy was all geared though toward achieving it. Every move was calculated and strategic. My books, articles, keynotes, and web profile are designed to show expertise in dealing with people, particularly those in management. My job is to get the message out that I have something important to share with the world. Through networking, I'm confident this goal will be realized although it will of course take time. But it's given me a guide and that's helped me go after certain business and turn down other stuff. The BHAG is my career strategic plan.

So how are you doing? Can you identify a BHAG? If so, have you mapped out a process to achieve it? I know plenty of people who can talk a good game and wow us with their dream, but this is only valid if you believe you can do it and you have a plan (which you work) to actually achieve it.

The following may be helpful as you think about establishing a BHAG. Your BHAG should be SMART!

- **S – Specific.** Make sure you're very clear on what the BHAG is. Remember, it has to be a mechanism to get the end state, not the end state itself.

- **M – Measurable.** Can you measure happiness? Wealth? Whatever you make your BHAG, be sure you can measure it so you know when you're getting close.

- **A – Adaptable.** What happens if the dream gets derailed? Will you be able to adapt your BHAG? If I got horribly disfigured, my Plan B would be a radio show instead. What's your backup plan?

- **R – Realistic.** There's a fine line between BHAG and Realistic. If you tell me your BHAG is to be a brain surgeon, but then quickly follow that with your low interest in math and science, the medical condition that causes your hands to shake uncontrollably, and the fact that you faint at the site of blood, I'm going to be skeptical. You won't be cutting into my brain! Rather than talk a good game, be realistic and go after that which you can *actually* achieve.

- **T – Trackable.** Can you measure your progress over time? Why not draw a model like the one I did using the mountain and switchbacks? This is a good way to evaluate career and job choices. See if your opportunity is a move up the mountain or back down a few steps. Be sure you're always moving forward and up!

A life without clear goals has the hidden danger of passing you by quickly. Take some time to think about your own goals and help others develop them too. Delegation is your best tool to reach them. You can delegate tasks that help someone else reach a BHAG.

How do you know much management to put into delegation? Take a look at the following diagram:

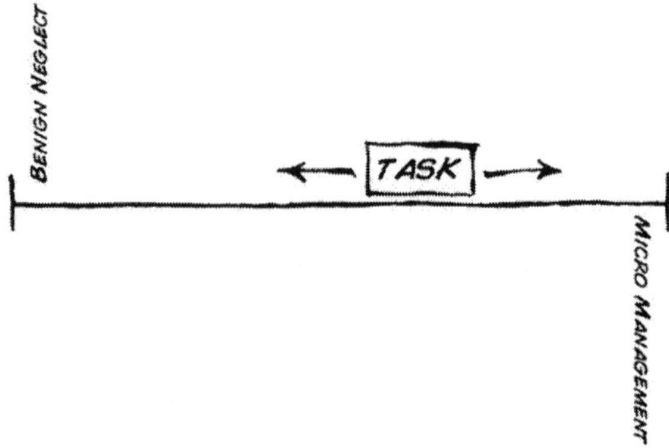

This took is a visual that shows a continuum. On one end is micromanagement, a term all of us are familiar with and all of us loath (even though some of you who are reading this are probably considered to be micromanagers by your team...) and on the other side is benign neglect. Both are harmful. How do you use this tool? Think about what it takes to teach the task.

If I was in Afghanistan visiting the troops and wanted to learn how to diffuse a roadside bomb, I'd want that Navy Explosive Ordnance Disposal (EOD) specialist to tell me EXACTLY what to do! Micromanage me all you want! On the other hand, eventually I'd want to try it on my own. I'd want some autonomy. If that EOD specialist told me to figure it out and then ran away with his fingers in his ears, that would be benign neglect.

Start delegating closer to the right side of the line. As the person gets more confident, give them some freedom. When they can do it without your direct supervision and have the ability to not only do the task but teach it to other, then officially assign it to them. Of course you'll always have the accountability for it, but at least you'll be helping them grow and give yourself some room to grow too.

Wow, that's a lot of material on performance management but I promise you it's worth the effort to implement. People will engage if they think what they do really matters and that you care about them. It takes time but it's time well spent. Are you ready to get started?

Your Strategy:

Get back in the habit of setting (and co-setting) performance goals and objectives.

Yes, it needs to be a habit. Do it constantly not just when HR says it's due.

Set up regular intervals to meet individually with them to evaluate progress.

Certainly use a formal process to do this, but don't wait if something needs to be fixed right away. I work with a lot of organizations that have a five-point scale for performance and complain about low performers. If you do regular meetings, you should NEVER have someone get the lowest rating. Either they should have fixed it when it happened or you should have already fired them.

Use coaching and feedback to grow strong performance and fix poor performance.

It's all performance management. Both tools are necessary and require constant use. Make it happen!

Points to Ponder

1. Do you have a performance management system at work that you're not optimizing? Are you using it for more than just a paper appraisal or is that it?

2. Think about your superstars. Are you recognizing their great performance frequently and not just waiting for appraisal time to do it?

3. What gaps are you identifying in your staff? Are you looking for ways to fill those gaps?

Chapter 9 – Show Some Empathy!

A few years ago I was facilitating a coaching workshop for a bunch of contractors at Fort Polk in Louisiana. This was an interesting group, made up of folks who made a living blowing things up. Their job was to construct lifelike battlefield simulations for the Army troops who were being sent off to Iraq and Afghanistan.

We began discussion the challenges between balancing work and family and if personal issues ever had the right to impact work. Of course in their field it helped to have a team focused at all times, considering any misstep could result in somebody getting killed or severely injured.

The group then shared a great tool with me that they used to help them manage this very important issue. I call it the ***Cubic Donut*** (which they allowed me to share provided I name it after them and their company, *Cubic Applications International*). Take a look at the diagram on the next page:

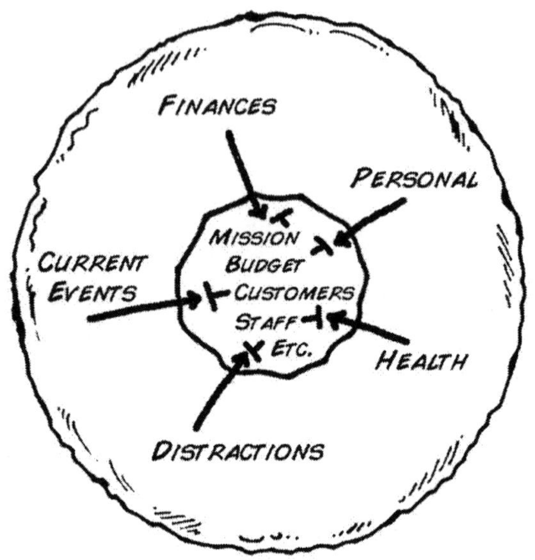

According to these folks, people have all sorts of issues that distract them all day. That's fine – after all, we give our employers our very best hours when you think about it.

On the other hand, managers need to focus on the business of the business – which includes things like the mission, the budget, customers, etc. When an employee's personal issue begins to impact their work and it affects the stuff in the "donut hole," it's time to take action and kick them out of the hole, not unlike a goalie in a hockey game.

Interestingly enough, these rough dudes didn't just kick people out of the office empty-handed. They had a comprehensive list of resources addressing nearly every issue the employees brought in. There were phone numbers to the Employee Assistance Program (EAP), debt counselors, marriage therapists, etc. Nobody got kicked out of the "donut hole" without a resource. Also, the managers were always diligent about following up to see how things were going. Nobody was left out in the cold and yet the managers didn't have a steady line of employees standing outside the office who needed personal help. It was a very effective system!

In these tough economic times, you can bet your staff experiences stress at home which just increases the challenges at work. If people give you the best eight hours of their day, don't expect them to leave their problems at home.

While your job is not to be a therapist or life coach, you can certainly provide a listening ear and provide resources to them if they need them. Take time to be sensitive if your staff seems preoccupied by personal problems, and then take quick steps to recommend help.

It may also be helpful to think about the difference between sympathy and empathy.

Sympathy is a surface expression of emotion usually done in response to some kind of tough challenge or issue. For example, if you watch those *Seinfeld* reruns, you often see Jerry and his friends eating at the coffee shop. If the server happens to trip and fall, Jerry's response is usually:

"Aw that's a shame..."

Not very helpful is it? It's sympathy, plain and simple. Here are some other examples of **sympathetic** responses:

- *I'm sorry*
- *That's too bad*
- *That's a shame*
- *Bummer*
- *It must suck to be you*

Let's see what it looks like in action:

Sympathy

Manager: "Chad you look bummed. What's wrong?"

Chad: "My dog just died."

Manager: "I'm sorry."

Chad: "Me too. Rover was my best friend."

Manager: "Hey when are you going to have that report finished? It's due at noon."

Not a lot of feeling is there? Sympathy typically doesn't help at all.

And then there's empathy. **Empathy** is getting linked into the emotion somebody is feeling, either by testing it first, then reacting, or just by tuning in. It's much deeper than sympathy. Some call it "putting yourself into another's shoes" which makes sense too. Take a look at the following example to find some empathy.

Empathy (Take 1)

> **Manager:** "Chad you look bummed. What's wrong?
>
> **Chad:** "My dog just died."
>
> **Manager:** "Oh my gosh, I know exactly how you feel! My dog died last month. He was the best dog, always loyal and I just cried and cried...."
>
> **Chad:** "Um, ok..."

Did you like that? Probably not. Keep in mind empathy is relating to somebody else's need, not reflection on your own. When you feel the temptation to insert your own experience in, pinch yourself! It's not about you!

Let's try it again

Empathy (Take 2)

> **Manager:** "Chad you look bummed. What's wrong?
>
> **Chad:** "My dog just died"
>
> **Manager:** "Oh my gosh, you must feel awful. Is everything ok?"
>
> **Chad:** "Yeah"
>
> **Manager:** "Tell me, were you really attached to your dog?"
>
> **Chad:** "No, actually I hated that mutt but my kids loved him and it breaks my heart to see them hurting."

See the difference? Test the feeling before just jumping in with your own bright ideas. It's all about the other person when it comes to expressing empathy. It takes practice too so you might want to practice using some scenarios of your own.

And by the way, if you're not normally sincere, be prepared to have your empathetic statements rejected. You'll have to build (or rebuild) some of that trust. Do it though, it's well worth the effort.

In my workshops, I always share this word of advice with the attendees:

People don't care about how much you know. They want to know how much you care.

Keep that in mind as you help your employees through their toughest times.

Your Strategy:

Develop a ready reference of solutions (i.e. counselors, EAP numbers, HR, etc.)

This shouldn't take you long to compile. It wouldn't hurt to share these resources with your peers either.

Take time to listen when they have problems, but quickly hand them the resource they need and get them back to work.

Remember, you're not a therapist or counselor. If you do enjoy this part of the job, consider doing it as a second career but for now, you have to take care of business. Refer back to the *Cubic Donut.*

Follow up as appropriate to check their progress.

Don't hand off resources and just leave people on their own. You do have a responsibility to ensure their safety, personal health, and sanity. Keep checking in and make sure they're following the plan you laid out for them.

Be a good listener – listen actively.

This means do less talking and more listening. Here's a helpful guide: W.A.I.T.

- **W** – Why
- **A** – Am
- **I** – I
- **T** – Talking?

Many organizations claim their people are the most valuable asset. If you truly believe this, you'll do what you can to take care of your superstars. What do you think?

Points to Ponder

1. Do you have a ready list of helpful personal resources for your team?

2. Are you a good empathizer or just a sympathizer? Do you always have to talk about yourself?

3. Do you really, REALLY care about your people?

Chapter 10 – *"To Infinity, and Beyond!"*

Imagine being on a luxury cruise ship, standing on the railing at night with your sweetheart looking at the water. As you gazing off into the moonlight, you see something in the water out of the corner of your eye. It's a lifeboat heading away from your cruise ship with the crew paddling frantically. As you look closer, you realize it's the ship's captain and all the ship's officers. What do you do?

Get off the ship as soon as possible! When the crew bails out, you just know trouble is on the way.

Are you creating this scenario right now in your own organization? Without hope and a future, your best performers will not stay with you. I know I wouldn't!

The whole purpose of engagement is to get your superstars to stay with you during tough times. In many cases, their loyalty may not be rewarded for months, or even years. Bonuses and raises might be put off indefinitely. If you don't give them hope of a happy ending, why should they bother to stay with you?

Think about people who have inspired hope over the years. Martin Luther King comes to mind as he envisioned a new future of equality for all races. Ronald Reagan spoke of us being "better off than we were four years ago." These were messages of hope and they sold. People made the commitment. We've seen it work over and over, and also seen the strategy of LACK of hope work as well. If there's no future, there's no commitment.

When people's sense of security is threatened, they respond by contracting their efforts. If you see your organization surviving the current economic challenges and coming out stronger, let your team know this and get them talking about what life will look like then. People will feel much more confident in their efforts if you tell them you fully expect to survive and want them around with you when the good times return.

Your Strategy:

Have frequent discussions about current progress in the organization.

Are you taking time to share good news with your employees? Conversely, are you letting them know about the bad stuff too? People need to be informed. If I know the ship is sinking but there are things I can do to prevent it, I'll get busy doing them! If I don't know, how can I help?

Meet with your team periodically and engage them on a discussion on how to maximize this downturn to set up future success.

Sometimes the best ideas come from the most unlikely sources. Everyone in your organization has great ideas. If you're not listening to them, or worse, not even asking them, how will you find out? Your company's salvation could be right in front of you and you don't even know it! Engage people in discussion if you want to engage them.

Speak to them as if they'll have great things to look forward to when the crisis abates.

When people see you hopeful, they'll be hopeful too. Visualize and communicate what life will look like in a better economy. Talk about what it will be like to be so busy you'll be turning down business. Happy days will come again and you'll need to get them pumped up in preparation.

Even when good economic times return, there's a good bet we'll see bad ones again. When bad times come back, good times will be just around the corner. What is the constant? Your superstars! They'll be with you every step of the way if you just engage them. Work each day to get them committed to you for the long haul.

Points to Ponder

1. When was the last time you spent some time engaging your team on strategic plans or initiatives? Do they really feel like part of the team?

2. Are you inspirational enough to get people engaged in the future of your organization? If not, take some time to study the most influential leaders of the 20th century and model them!

Chapter 11 – Final Thoughts

About 25 years ago, I worked with a young and attractive woman who was married to a much older man. She was vivacious and driven, having many goals and dreams on her agenda. She worked in a very tiring job and pursued her college degree by attending school in the evenings and on weekends. Her husband was extremely jealous and controlling, and although she never entertained a thought about other men, he insisted she must be cheating on him. He began stalking her, even feeling the hood of her car to see if she'd been out and tracking the odometer reading to check her stories out.

He laughed at her dreams of getting a degree and her career aspirations. Part of it was jealousy, part just stupidity. Finally, frustrated by the lack of trust, persistent accusations, and eventually some physical abuse, she left him.

From what I hear today, she is an extremely successful manager with a great career, nice home, attractive family, and a never-ending string of good fortune. Her organization sees her as a superstar and her family does too. She is engaged and loyal to her organization and career because she is surrounded by people who care and who demonstrate it.

If her Ex was around, he'd probably regret taking her for granted and for keeping her locked away. Then again, he was a moron so he'd most likely repeat the same behaviors.

If you have superstars, are you building them up or attempting to hide them away? The tighter you hold onto them, the more likely they are to slip from your grasp. Develop them, appreciate them, communicate with them, love them, and use them to their full capacity and they'll be loyal to the end.

The steps in the book are simple, yet not simplistic. Are you prepared to do what it takes to implement them? I hope so. Remember, every bad economy leads into a good one and the good eventually goes bad. The one constant is the superstar employee. Will yours be there for you?

Hopefully you found this book to be education, inspirational, and practical. If you did, then put the principles into action. After all, inspiration is just potential energy. It's only released when we take steps to apply it. Please take time to read the *Points to Ponder* and respond to them. Develop a roadmap for yourself and use this book as one of your tools to move ahead. Surround yourself with smart people and work hard to be an inspiration to others around you.

I hope you'll keep in touch and let me know how you're doing. As one who may have started you on this journey, I also have the responsibility to see you through. Let me know how things are going and if I may ever be of assistance to you! You can always contact me through my website at ***MackMunro.com.***

I won't wish you luck, because luck is yours to create. I will however wish you well in your journey!

Endeavor to Persevere!

Mack Munro
April 1, 2019

The principles in my book will only work for you if you put them into practice. What are you waiting for?

Mack Munro

Appendix
Survey Findings

Methodology

While much research on workplace turnover reveals people essentially "quitting their boss," our findings reveal much deeper reasons. Additionally, the personal relationship findings show very similar driving forces.

This study involved sending two separate online surveys over a two-week period. The survey links were broadcast via social media nation-wide. The first survey asked for respondents to identify the number one reason they quit a job where they had been tenured at least one year. Respondents were asked to identify their gender and age. Additionally, they were able to make specific comments.

The second survey asked respondents to identify the number one reason they ended a personal relationship that was at least three years in duration. Respondents were asked to identify their gender and age. They were also able to make specific comments.

Job Survey Numbers

Job Survey Question

The NUMBER ONE reason I left my job was...

- You were underemployed (job was boring)
- The job was too stressful
- There were no opportunities for growth or promotion
- A better opportunity knocked elsewhere
- You couldn't stand your boss
- Management put a freeze on raises and promotions
- Management constantly reorganized, shuffled people around, and changed strategic direction
- No recognition
- Difficult company culture
- Poor pay and benefits
- Other (please specify)*

* These responses were manually evaluated and placed in the existing category. This was possible in nearly every response.

Respondents by Gender

144 Females	**65%**
76 Males	**35%**

Why Women Leave a Job

Difficult company culture	**32%**
There were better opportunities elsewhere	**22%**
No opportunities for growth or promotion	**20%**

Difficult company culture

- I was asked to do something that was immoral
- Managing partner was bi-polar and constantly reorganized, gave tasks and took them away, and gradually drove away key clients with her "attitude" and pricing strategies. After losing a major client, we were all told we were suddenly hourly employees and would be paid based on income generated, but when it came time to be paid, this partner would find excuses to delay - each time it was because one client or another had not

paid their bill for the prior month. I eventually contacted a couple of clients and set up my own office. Would prefer to be working with a law firm but the older I get, the harder that is to imagine.

- Environment was too structured.
- Combination of the above, but elected to take time off to heal and reassess what was next for me.
- Long hours, overworked
- Management and ownership were nuts!
- Company wasn't financially sound
- Poor Management.
- Burnt out of dealing with several of the things listed above.
- Hours -- weekends and night
- It was a second job and not worth the stress
- An abusive boss who wanted me to falsely certify 401k tax returns
- The culture wasn't professional enough & in the end it didn't align with my long-term professional career goals
- The ethics of the company changed
- Management favoring certain employees visible by many
- I left because the "manager" wasn't and the owner did not think women belonged in the workplace...

- I was being mistreated, harassed, and discriminated against, etc.
- Short staffed all the time and management didn't address it
- I was asked to do something that I considered unethical
- Lack of support and either no processes in place where needed or no follow through/adherence to policy
- This particular job was extremely uncomfortable due to personalities in the office. I wasn't the only one who thought that. I'd have to say my boundaries were challenged, and it was impossible to thrive. Moving on was the best decision!
- I was asked to allow cheating on a test
- no appreciation for the hard work and dedication
- Jobs will promise you one thing and then do something totally different. Usually I would stay to see what the company offered but on this particular job when I asked others about the promises made, they had been there 2-4 years waiting for things promised to take place.
- I asked for 2 years during the budget season for help in the department...ignored, and unfortunately, I was a workaholic by

then, could not cut back services......so I retired early and left a 23-year job

- Company was sold twice in one month and hours were cut substantially
- Post-acquisition the entire corporate culture changed. It was no longer pleasant there.
- Due to change in companies and management, staffing and supplies decreased leading to decreased patient care.
- I found out about protocols and directives at the same time my employees did. This made it very difficult to do my job and manage people through new directives when I was still asking questions myself and orienting myself to the new policies.
- I was working for a company that was in significant financial turmoil. Much as I enjoyed what I did and the people I worked with, it was time to move into a more stable opportunity.
- It was also too stressful; I was a customer service manager and working over 12 hours a day so I had no time for my family.
- Company culture came in a close second as I need to have an ethical and open business environment in which to grow.

- Too little pay for too much work. Responsibilities constantly increased without compensation. Working 70+ hours a week and getting paid for 40. Constantly expected to work during time off and vacations.
- My boss took credit for my work and stifled my ability to grow.
- My boss always left me stupid notes signed with a "cat" because they are her favorites but it was always when she would find a mistake instead of telling me....I could predict when I would get a note and finally the last straw, I saw another note in the morning and after taking my 1st call, I went in to another mgr and told her I was leaving; thankfully I was called back to the same company working for the general mgr. and for the great company that it was; I think she learned a lesson after that from what I could see.
- It's usually office politics. Illegal underhandedness on the part of supervisors or Human Resources. They utilize temp. agencies to circumvent employees having legal standing.
- Boss was an alcoholic and only viewed women as a prize and not for business. Friends with too many he knew were

taking advantage of him, but he (boss) allowed it. Stated in order to increase me pay he would have to increase the only other female employee's pay. I increased profits by $2 million in less than one year (Jan-July) and then he took all office personnel to Mexico 2 months after I quit.

- My idea of the health care mission is to help patients. It seemed their mission was to raise MD productivity to bill more. Never seemed to measure clinical outcomes -- just how much $ could be put on the books
- Too many chiefs not enough Indians
- My boss micromanaged and only offered negative feedback in the form of screaming at employees
- Very poor management. My boss had no idea what she was doing. Spent all her time on smoke breaks. Could not properly train any of us and we ended up learning on our own. There was no team work and this job depended on each other doing steps for the next person. Just horrible!
- In all companies, the management team should keep personal personal and business business. The company I worked for would cut your hours if they

did not like you. But, they hired that person. Also instead of promoting from within , they would bring in outside help instead of giving the qualified workers a chance that they already had. They have a buddy system, and them pay them more than everybody else. That's why workers stop doing their job completely, then it falls back on others

- I have had issues 3 times in my career with organizations who refuse to comply with various laws and who wanted me to sign off on dishonest practices. This is a common problem for HR people. I know of several who had to quit jobs for similar reasons; you also lose your professional certification if it is found out that you've behaved unethically
- difficult company culture that expected people to devote all of their free time to work
- I was a professor teaching Ph.D. and Masters Students and was told I needed to "pass" failing students (who were not qualified to be in the program to begin with) because of their race. I quit instead
- The company I left was in Chapter 11 and I might have hung out to hope for the best but the company shifted my job

to a position that I did not care for which made the job stressful

- It was a State job at a local community college and there was far too much political garbage going on and not enough work
- My job was extremely demanding and I feel I could've handled that better if my boss were supportive. Instead, my boss was deeply insecure to the point where she would talk behind your back every time you were out sick or you made a mistake. A huge layer of stress that wasn't necessary.
- Really, all of the above. Mgmt. could not be trusted, put people in positions that were not qualified but refused to listen to workers' reason to improve, appeared insincere and not willing to accept wise counsel, implemented programs and quickly implemented another in its place without giving time/thought to determine the success of the previous, lack of recognition for individual success, created a culture of active mistrust
- Having difficulty landing a job in my new career path - definite age discrimination out there which is WRONG!

- Being involved in retail it is difficult to obtain any position that is not management as full time. When promised a set amount of hours when hired and then your hours are lowered do to overstaffing, favoritism or bad economy makes it difficult to not only survive as a single person, but makes it even harder to plan ahead for important things such as paying bills, etc. I have found retail as a who you know job situation more than what you know and I am talking about experience and education versus if your best friend is the boss!
- My job was also very stressful, which lead to health concerns.

There were better opportunities elsewhere

- to pursue a different career path
- Needed full time so looked and went elsewhere
- There were more attractive options outside the corporate world
- My manager was distrustful of his reports, petty, and 100% 'by the book' no matter what the situation. I couldn't stand him. During the last 2 weeks of my engagement, he was replaced by a

wonderful human being. I had already begun negotiations with another company. Though my new manager was fully aware of the contemptible things that had been going on, and begged me to stay to help him 'fix' the practice, I was committed to leaving. So I truly quit because I found a better opportunity.

- I have quit multiple jobs over the years - usually for a better opportunity. My answer above was for the one time I quit because I just could not stand to continue in the job. Our company was acquired and they stripped the staff to bare bones with the plan to make the numbers look good and re-sell (we did not know this until later when they did not sell). I was put in a position that was a stretch for me, responsible for way too much with way too few staff.
- My boss was never at work and didn't mind dumping her work on me but I never got the credit
- New supervisor came on board and started reorganization of HR dept. without getting to know the culture/people; structure would not support the business partners; stress caused many to leave and she replaced

everyone with unqualified but quality people in all promotional opportunities

- Having returned to a position as a part timer that I'd previously been 'Manager of' - the 'then' Manager decided to MICRO manage everyone, even those who'd done the job for years and KNEW what they were doing -- it was very demeaning and worthless. The previous two 'managers' (as they had three to do the job I left full-time) were fine. They respected our knowledge and ability and let us DO the job...the third one did not. She was less experienced and less educated than those already there and clearing insecure.
- I left for better benefits and more hours.
- There are many times a position hired into does not pan out to be the job you envisioned and therefore unfulfilling. You can have the conversation about your true talents but they don't tap into them for one reason or another, leaving the person frustrated to not being able to be the absolute best they can be for the organization.
- Found a much better paying position that better utilizes my skills.

No opportunities for growth or promotion

- Not using my skills appropriately; not enough personal satisfaction
- There were multiple reasons for leaving the job [boring, no advancement opportunities, low pay], but the number one reason was boredom.
- I had an 11-year career and left the company on excellent terms to pursue a start-up opportunity basically an offer I could not refuse was presented
- Only way to advance is to buy the business.

Why Men Leave a Job

Better opportunities elsewhere	**37%**
Difficult company culture	**31%**
Couldn't stand my boss	**28%**

Better opportunities elsewhere

- Wanted to grow and learn in another opportunity
- There were no opportunities to obtain a stake in the company as initially discussed when I interviewed for the job.
- I left Microsoft back in 2000 for exactly 5 weeks when they called me back to work

for them. I originally only left due to more money.

- Pay Freeze was also in place for 4 years. Had opportunity to go elsewhere & do the same work for better money & Better Benefits
- I decided I could do better going out on my own as an independent contractor, so I turned my employer into a client, then added other clients -- which gave me more flexibility and satisfaction but less financial security. I wish I'd done it sooner.
- The pay and benefits were higher and I was somewhat dissatisfied with the fact that I had been passed over for a management position.
- I have left jobs before because of stress, no recognition, poor boss and no growth
- Although most of the above answers are true, it wasn't until a better opportunity came along that I finally left.
- Compensation expectations were not met over 5 years
- After 5 years of very satisfied employment and success, I had a great new opportunity present itself.
- No opportunity to become vested in the company and truly share in the growth of the company so that I would have

something to show for my efforts at the end.
- Needed an opportunity for growth

Difficult company culture

- Gov't contracting is much like prostitution, You know what is the right thing to do, but you are forced to do the wrong thing by politically motivated leadership.
- Lack of recognition
- Wrong peer group - values and interests a poor match
- When I worked for an insurance company, the job was too stressful.
- High stress, high profile job, lacking (BUT NOT "No") appreciative recognition
- Failure to recognize required operating guidelines, no integrity by leadership.
- Employer spoke in loud voice about fellow colleague while this person was in a room with customer. Secondly employer treated many customers badly and they refused to return. The customer would inform the professional that referred them to this office as to the terrible service received. Thus causing professional to call questioning our service

- Lack of Integrity
- Working with good people is everything.
- I've quit 5 jobs, and mostly it's because the culture is not positive. Poor (or no) raises, no recognition, and managers who don't know how to encourage and support!
- Leadership change came and disrupted everything that was in place. New leadership meant that new people were brought in and the current employees were moved along or made to feel that they didn't fit the new culture or executive team.
- Too much oversight; not enough freedom to exercise judgment; unnecessary meetings
- It was a combination of company culture, an ineffective president, bad management decisions and a pay freeze (potential cuts) while spending was rampant in other areas.
- Family owned business run by the saying My Way or the Highway! Threats, intimidation and a culture of lies, deceit and mistrust
- The employcr would state how important the customer was to the business, but didn't always treat them as so, but would expect front office staff to treat them as

gold and take care of damage control. Poor leadership. Degraded employees for continuing education.

- Small, growing internet children's education business. Owner became obsessed and overextended. Beyond salvage.
- Married couple could not get along and they were both my boss. The company finally split.
- While the stress was several years before my leaving, it left a stain on my outlook toward my work... I had to move on to feel fulfilled
- The company culture lead to promoting only certain types of people. Those full supported the top down management style. So even though I has very productive, I was perceived as a poor worker because I did not follow the same methodology they wanted
- In addition, the company made it impossible to earn any pay. Quotas were raised mid-month in order for me not to achieve my goals.
- After confirming business process shortcomings (identified during the interview process) during the first week on the job, the CEO invited me to be part of the "misdirection" (actual word used)

necessary to grow the Company. Hence, I knew my tenure would be short since there would be inevitable conflict, and also (as I subsequently discovered additional questionable practices) that I had no desire to spend my retirement in Fort Leavenworth

- Couldn't stand my boss
- I've had some horrible bosses.
- He constantly changed direction, was not strategic. Nice person but VERY hard to work for. High Turnover
- The new boss (a replacement) focused on personalities, not concerns. He took everyone back to a very "high school" kind of experience.
- I was in a management position and a rival got a promotion over me. I now work for him and it is not pleasant so I am looking to leave
- There were a number of reasons I could have chosen above, including being underemployed, no room for growth or promotion, no recognition and difficult company culture, but all of these were encompassed by having a poor boss who was not willing to rectify (or fight to rectify) any of these situations on behalf of his/her employees.

Relationship Survey Numbers

Respondents by Gender

94 Females	**67%**
46 Males	**33%**

Relationship Survey Question
The NUMBER ONE reason I ended my personal relationship was...

- My partner wasn't as serious about the relationship as I was
- Inability to manage or resolve conflict
- My partner couldn't manage money
- My partner tried to control me
- My partner and I couldn't communicate
- My partner had no interest in growing intellectually
- My partner and I had differing career goals
- Frankly, someone better came along that I was more compatible with
- My partner was abusive
- My partner failed to live up to what they promised (in our goals as a couple)
- My partner's religious beliefs, cultural and lifestyle differences were inflexible

- My partner was cheating on me (physically and/or emotionally)
- My partner had no interest in enhancing our relationship
- Other (please specify)*

* These responses were manually evaluated and placed in the existing category. This was possible in nearly every response.

Why Women Leave Relationships

My partner was cheating on me (physically and/or emotionally)	**22%**
My partner had no interest in enhancing our relationship	**13%**
My partner tried to control me	**8%**

My partner cheated on me

- Several of the above, it all added up to be too much cheating, he had no interest in fixing out relationship, couldn't communicate, couldn't manage conflict
- Had an affair before the kids; some abuse that husband was unwilling to admit was wrong to do; wife/kids (family)

My partner had no interest in enhancing our relationship

- My partner didn't pay enough attention to me. I felt like a widow.
- He lost all passion for life
- I was doing the work; he was never instigating anything or trying to share

time. The friends/family were always more important.

Why Men Leave Relationships

Frankly, someone better came along that I was more compatible with	**19%**
My partner failed to live up to what they promised (in our goals as a couple)	**16%**
My partner was cheating on me (physically and/or emotionally)	**10%**

My partner failed to live up to what they promised (in our goals as a couple)

- We just grew apart; as time went on we had less and less in common
- I was content, but not happy. Social interactions with friends (as a couple) were lacking and her sexual desire level had dramatically decreased.
- Frankly, someone better came along that I was more compatible with relationship
- Being alone is a better alternative.

Analysis

Finding #1: Human Beings are "Wired" for Relationships

In both studies, the major reasons people moved on was the feeling of being abandoned or wronged by either the partner or the organization. In personal relationships a need wasn't met, but the need appeared to be less tangible, and more related to a feeling of the other partner not living up to a commitment. In the employment relationship, the reasons for moving on centered on a lack of commitment toward the individual's career intentions and from a difficult work environment.

In relationships, people seem to build a tolerance to less-than-optional situations but then it does appear that one major event causes them to leave. With men, it seems as though a sustained pattern of dissatisfaction leads them to seek out a new relationship. With females, it was one major even that caused them to leave and most women were more tolerant of other issues. The other issues focused on a more unhealthy relationship environment that was dissatisfying but not intolerable. Perhaps they had more patience.

People are emotional beings and the workplace is often an extension of that emotional context. Where people feel cheated, ignored, or disrespected, their tendency is to move from that relationship.

Finding #2:
Human Beings are constantly on the Lookout for Better Opportunities for Personal and Professional Benefit

One implied but perhaps never formally mentioned aspect of the employer-employee agreement is that of professional development. People go into jobs with the intent of deriving continuous growth. While the trend today is to stay in a job for three years before leaving for another job, most people it seems would prefer to stay in a company where they would constantly be challenged and afforded new opportunities to learn new skills and take on higher levels of responsibilities. When a ceiling appears, people see that as a sign of capping out at that level and immediately look for a new opportunity.

In our study, this is the number one reason people moved on. Men and women both sought a chance to grow and found none.

Finding #3:
Men and Women need a positive working environment to remain engaged.

Since human beings spend the majority of their waking hours with an employer, they should expect a professional and at a minimum, collegial environment. People have an expectation for fairness from their boss, co-workers who treat each other with respect, and environment free of harmful conflict and discontent.

In our study, this was the number one reason for women to leave an organization and the number two reason for men.

Working in a positive culture is a significant driver of employee retention and satisfaction. Depending on the severity of the situation, a person may leave even if they love what they do and are well compensated.

Finding #4:
Compensation has little effect on employee engagement

Most studies that analyze employee engagement find compensation as a fairly insignificant driver. Managers tend to view compensation as a high contributor to commitment, but that appears to be changing. Our research showed pay and benefits as the lowest of all identified reasons for quitting in both genders. It was only identified as the number one driver in 20-29-year-old males.

Compensation and benefits are important, but as a factor in driving engagement and retention, they are among the least significant.

Motivation comes when people get what they need, when they need it.

Mack Munro

About the Author

Mack Munro is Founder and CEO of **Boss Builders** and is an experienced speaker and consultant, and who has worked with executive and management teams in companies of all types, sizes, and industries in the USA and abroad. He is the author of *How to Be a Great Boss* and three other business books.

He holds a Master of Arts degree in Organizational Leadership from Chapman University and a Bachelor of Science degree in Health Care Management from Southern Illinois University He is a qualified facilitator of the Myers-Briggs Type Indicator® and has also written and developed a number of personality and behavioral assessments and online tools.

Mack's background is primarily in Healthcare, Manufacturing, Consulting, Information Technology, Entrepreneurship, Leadership & Management, and Marketing. His typical clients come from these areas.

Prior to starting his company, Mack created training and professional development programs at U.T. Medical Group, Inc. in Memphis, TN,

Holy Cross Hospital in Silver Spring, MD, and Contract Services Association of America in Arlington, VA. Mack has been an adjunct Professor of Business and Management at Vincennes University in Bremerton, WA and Crichton College in Memphis, TN. He a retired United States Navy dental technician who served tours in Australia, Guam, Long Beach, California, and Bremerton, Washington.

Mack has delivered keynotes to groups and associations around the country and internationally, and is a regular speaker at the Society for Human Resource Management (SHRM) state and local chapter meetings.

He has been featured as a career expert on radio, television, and printed and electronic media and hosts two podcasts, the ***HR Oxygen*** podcast and ***The Boss Builder Podcast***.

Stay Connected to Mack!

Blog: Mack maintains a blog with weekly postings on management, leadership, career development, and supervisory skills. View it and subscribe to the feed at:

www.MackMunro.com

***Twitter*:** Get regular notifications of updates to via Twitter. Follow Mack at:

www.twitter.com/thebossbuilders

***Facebook*:** Become one of Mack's *Facebook* Friends! Connect at:

www.facebook.com/thebossbuilders

LinkedIn: Connect on Mack's *LinkedIn* page to get access to his extensive network of professionals. Link in at:

www.linkedin.com/in/coachmunro

GREAT PERFORMANCE
SKILL
WILL
FOCUS

How Boss Builders Partners with You to Build Better Bosses

We have three options available to help you, the busy and stressed HR professional improve the competence and confidence of your company's managers.

Option #1: Our Onsite *Driving Results*® Instructor-Led Workshops

***Driving Results*® Onsite Workshops** are the most efficient way to train a small group of Bosses (between 10 and 30 participants) if you prefer live training at a location of your choosing.

This program, if delivered from start to finish, is four-days long. We can deliver it for you in half or one-day increments if you like.

Benefits:

- Interactive training and the opportunity for live skills practice.
- Opportunity to weave current participant challenges into the workshop.
- No travel expenses for attendees.

If you're interested in us bringing our training onsite to your organization, we are happy to oblige. Here is our standard course offering. Scroll to the very bottom for pricing.

Option #2: Our Boss Builder Academy Video Series

Boss Builder Academy is best for organizations that want to train multiple new Bosses.

- Boss Builder Academy kickoff (live or webinar) with a Boss Builder facilitator
- Structured guidelines for coaching and giving feedback to Boss Builder Academy participants by their manager
- Pre and Post Phase online evaluations to measure the growth and learning of the participants
- 12 month subscription to the video content
- Access to the *BossFlix*™ video library
- All worksheets and handouts for the videos and webinars.

Option #3: *Driving Results®* Curriculum License and Purchase

License and Materials

This license gives company the right to purchase and deliver our Driving Results workshops to your team. The license stays with your organization for as long as you like and does NOT transfer to any individual if they leave your company. Former employees can purchase a license in their new organization if they choose. This protects your investment.

The license gives you access to a robust instructor guide which includes a slide-by-slide video demonstration with suggestions on delivery techniques. You'll also have access to any product updates via a dedicated learning portal. A certified Boss Builder facilitator can be onsite to walk you through set-up or co-instruct with your trainers on a per-day basis. This rate is available when you open your quote as an option.

Each attendee must purchase a workbook and assessment which is priced per-user in the quote. These will be marked up in a class as there are many fill-in-the-blank areas.

For more information on how Boss Builders can help you develop better Bosses, contact us at:

Mack Munro
P.O. Box 75
Vanleer, TN 37181
(931) 221-2988
Mack@TheBossBuilders.com

BOSSBUILDERS

Made in the USA
Columbia, SC
15 March 2019